A Kid's Guide to
~~COVENTRY PUBLIC LIBRARY~~
Origami™

Making ORIGAMI ANIMALS Step by Step

Michael G. LaFosse

The Rosen Publishing Group's
PowerKids Press™
New York

To Richard L. Alexander, whose inspiration and creative ideas helped in the development of many of these wonderful projects.

Published in 2002 by The Rosen Publishing Group, Inc.
29 East 21st Street, New York, NY 10010

First Edition

Book Design: Emily Muschinske
Project Editors: Jennifer Landau, Jason Moring, Jennifer Quasha

Illustration Credits: Michael G. LaFosse
Photographs by Adriana Skura, background image of paper crane on each page © CORBIS.

LaFosse, Michael G.
Making origami animals step by step / Michael G. LaFosse.
     p. cm. — (A kid's guide to origami)
Includes bibliographical references and index.
  ISBN 0-8239-5877-9
1. Origami—Juvenile literature. 2. Animals in art—Juvenile literature. [1. Origami. 2. Animals in art. 3. Handicraft.]
I. Title. II. Series.
  TT870 .L234218 2002
  736'.982—dc21
                                                                                    2001001107

Manufactured in the United States of America

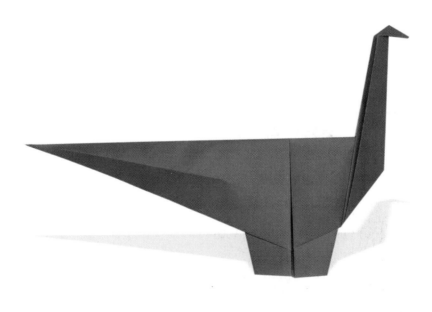

Contents

What Is Origami?

Origami, the Japanese art of paper folding, has been an important part of that country's **culture** for hundreds of years. In the Japanese language, "ori" means folding and "kami" means paper. In Japan, children learn origami at a young age. Origami uses a language of **symbols**, just like music. Once you know origami symbols, you can read an origami book from anywhere in the world.

All of the origami projects in this book are made from square-shaped paper. You do not need to buy special origami paper to do these projects. Just be sure the paper you use is square. It also must be the right size for the project you are making. When you start a project, make sure the paper faces in the same way as it does in the instructions.

You will enjoy making these origami animals. Imagine the living animal when you fold any of these projects. That way you will make lively sculptures, and each one will have its own

personality. Use the key on page 22 to help you make your origami projects. The key also explains terms such as <u>mountain fold</u> and <u>valley fold</u> that are used throughout the book.

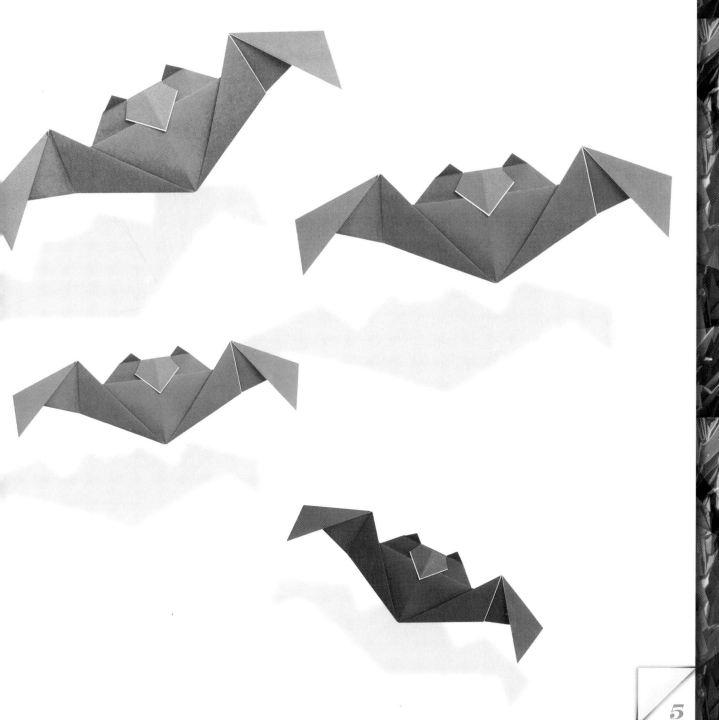

Butterfly

The butterfly is a great subject for an origami model. The wings of a butterfly are thin and beautifully colored, like origami paper. A butterfly begins its life as a caterpillar. After a while, the caterpillar finds a safe place to hide while it becomes a **chrysalis**. This is the stage where the caterpillar turns into a butterfly. When the time is right, the butterfly comes out from the shell of the chrysalis, dries its wings, and flies away.

1

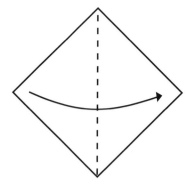

Use two squares of paper 8 inches (20.3 cm) wide or less. If you are using origami paper, start with the white side up. Fold the papers in half, corner to corner, to make triangles.

2

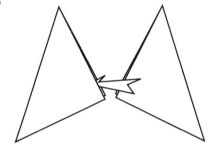

Fit one triangle into the other. Make the top two corners closer together than the bottom two corners.

3

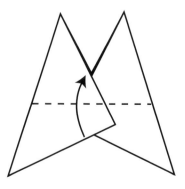

Fold the bottom half up. Match the two V-shaped openings.

4

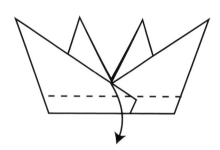

Fold down the two corners of the top layer.

5

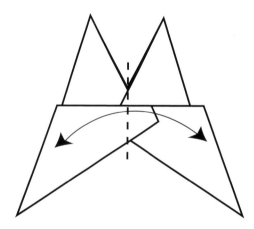

Fold in half and then unfold.

Bat

Bats are the only **mammals** that truly can fly. They are **nocturnal** creatures, meaning they are most active at night. Bats live to be about 15 years old, though some can live until 30.

Bats are symbols of good luck in China. Fold five red Bats to make a Chinese-style good-luck decoration. Five is the Chinese lucky number and red is the Chinese lucky color. Five red Bats are very lucky indeed!

1

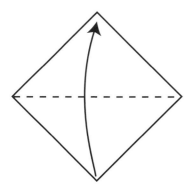

Use a square piece of paper 10 inches (25.4 cm) wide or less. If you are using origami paper, start with the white side up. Fold in half, corner to corner, to make a triangle.

2

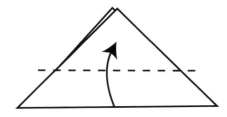

Fold up the bottom edge, but not to the top. Look at step three to see the correct shape.

3

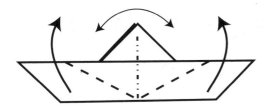

<u>Mountain fold</u> the paper in half, up the middle, and unfold. Fold up the two corners to form the wings.

4

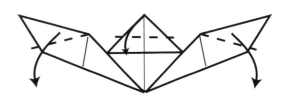

Fold down the middle corner. Fold down the two wing corners.

5

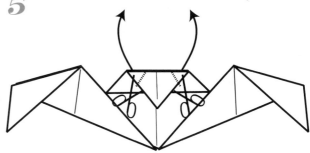

Cut two corners for ears and fold them up.

6

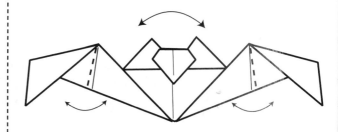

Fold and unfold the two wings at their middle point.

Cat

Here is an origami model that will please anyone who loves cats. You can change your origami Cat's personality by changing the size or the angle of its ears, the size of its **muzzle**, the shape of its nose, or the face that you draw on it. You can open its ears or mouth to bring it to life. This Cat likes to "eat" small, flat slips of paper and is a great way to give somebody a movie ticket, a special postage stamp, or even a reminder to clean the litter box. This Cat makes a good bookmark, too. Just let it hold onto the corner of the page with its mouth.

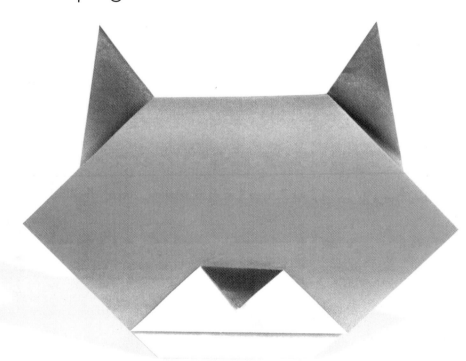

1

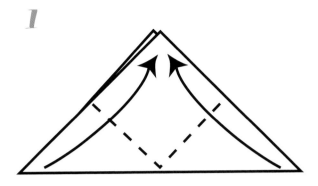

Use a square piece of paper 10 inches (25.4 cm) wide or less. If you are using origami paper, start with the white side up. Begin with the paper folded in half, corner to corner, like step one for the Bat. Carefully fold up the two side corners to the top corner.

2

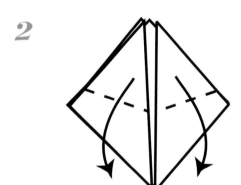

Fold down the two corners.

3

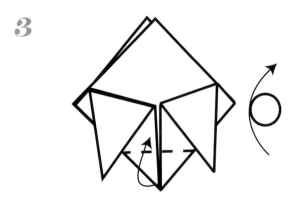

Fold up the middle corner. Turn the paper over so that it looks like the picture in step four.

4

Fold up the bottom corner of the top layer of paper. Look at step five to see the correct shape.

5

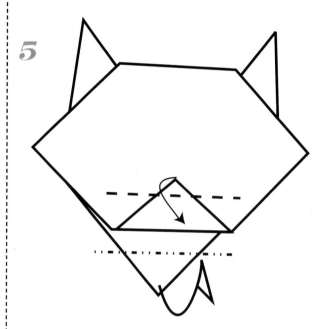

Fold down the tip of the corner to make a nose. <u>Mountain fold</u> the bottom corner behind the paper to form the Cat's chin.

Turtle

The turtle is a symbol for many things: long life, wisdom, and patience. Cultures that have great respect for their elders **revere** the turtle because it seems so old and wise. Turtles move slowly and have a tough shell to **discourage** other animals from eating them. There are many types of turtles. Some live in ponds and streams while others live in the sea. Turtles can live to be more than 100 years old.

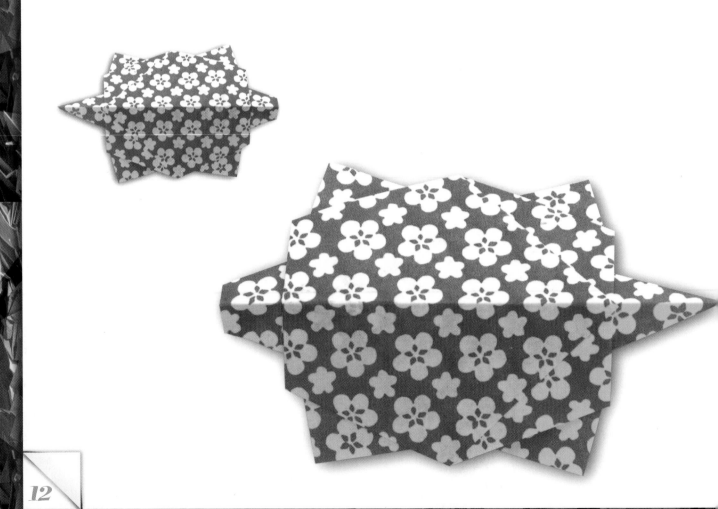

1

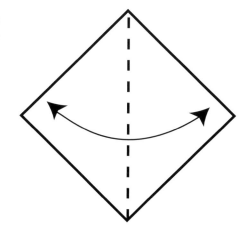

Use two square pieces of paper 10 inches (25.4 cm) wide or less. If you are using origami paper, start with the white side up. Fold each in half, corner to corner, and unfold.

2

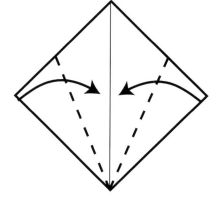

Fold two edges to the crease to make a kite shape. Do this with both papers.

3

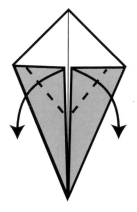

Fold down the two square corners of each paper.

4

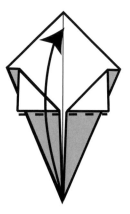

Fold up the bottom corner of each paper.

5

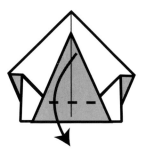

Fold down the corner so it falls below the bottom edge of the shape.

6

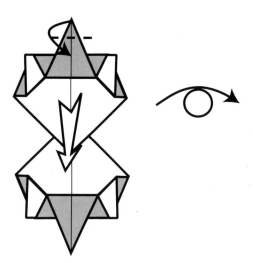

Fit the two pieces together. Fold down one corner to form the head. Turn the paper over.

Ducks

Springtime is like a new beginning. Each piece of paper that you fold is a new beginning, too. This origami mother and baby Duck is a great way to welcome spring. Fold this origami and paste it to a card. Then you will have a wonderful greeting card to send to friends and family.

Baby animals are a sure sign that spring has arrived, especially in areas that have cold winters. The warmth of spring frees the water, and plants begin to grow again. Living things need food and water, which are hard to find in the cold winter months. Some animals **hibernate** during this season, while others move to warmer places.

1

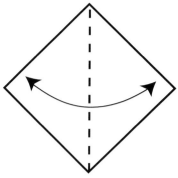

Use a square piece of paper 10 inches (25.4 cm) wide or less. If you are using origami paper, start with the white side up. Fold in half, corner to corner.

2

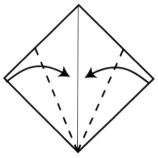

Carefully fold two edges to the crease to make a kite shape.

3

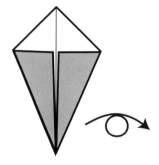

Turn over the paper.

4

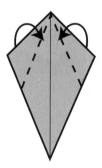

Fold in the two short edges of the kite to make a diamond shape.

5

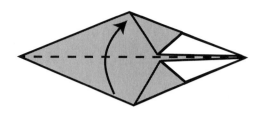

Turn the paper to look like the picture in this step. Fold up the bottom corner to the top.

6

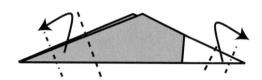

Valley fold and mountain fold each of the two end corners to form the neck and head of each Duck. Look at step seven for the correct shape.

7

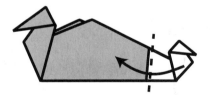

Fold over the baby Duck.

8

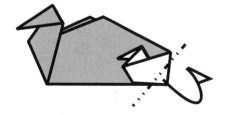

Mountain fold the back end of the baby Duck.

Skunk

Animals have different ways of keeping other animals from bothering them. The skunk can spray a powerful and **annoying** scent to discourage an attacker. This works even better with the skunk's bright white stripe acting as a warning label. Once a dog or a fox has been sprayed by an angry skunk, it is less likely to trouble another one. Animals far away can see the skunk's white warning stripe. The white stripe can even be seen at night, when most skunks are out digging for worms and **grubs**.

Fold your origami Skunk from paper that is black on one side and white on the other. This way your origami Skunk will look like the real animal. You may choose other colors as well. What's wrong with having a pink or a purple Skunk? Add a touch of perfume to the paper to make a scented Skunk.

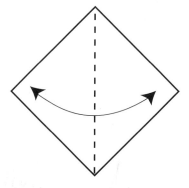

1

Use a square piece of paper 10 inches (25.4 cm) wide. If you are using origami paper, start with the white side up. Fold in half, corner to corner, and unfold.

2

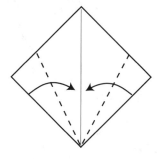

Carefully fold in the two bottom edges, but not to the crease line. Be sure to leave some white paper showing.

3

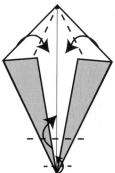

Fold in the two top edges. Leave some white paper showing. Fold up a little of the bottom corner for a nose, then fold up more of the bottom paper for the head.

4

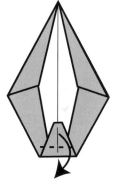

Fold down the head paper.

5

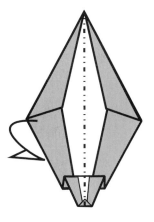

Mountain fold in half.

6

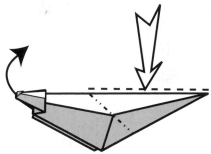

Pull up the head a little. Tuck in the tail paper and bend it down. Look at step seven to see the correct shape.

7

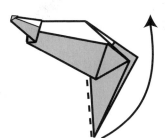

Fold up the tail paper.

8

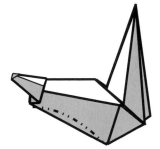

Mountain fold a curved line, from front to back, on each side, to make the four feet.

"Bobbin" the Fox

I named this little fox "Bobbin" because that is what his head will be doing once you put it together! Bobbin is an example of an action origami model. There are many kinds of action origami. There are birds that flap their wings, frogs that jump, and pinwheels that spin. Bobbin will delight anybody who sees that its head moves. You can make Bobbin nod "yes" or turn his head side to side for "no." The Bobbin shape is easy to teach to others, so you can share it often. Try placing Bobbin's head on your finger or on the corner of a book to make a friend smile.

1

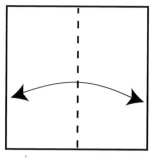

Use two square pieces of paper 6 inches (15.2 cm) wide or less. Use paper that is colored the same on both sides. Fold one piece in half, edge to edge. Open the paper up like a book.

2

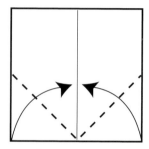

Fold in the two bottom corners to the crease.

3

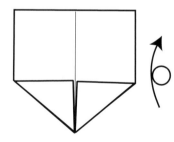

Turn the paper over, bottom to top.

4

Fold down the top point. Fold in the two bottom corners to the crease.

5

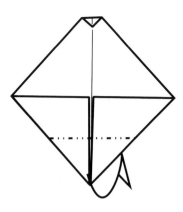

Mountain fold the bottom corner to the back. Make it touch the middle of the paper.

6

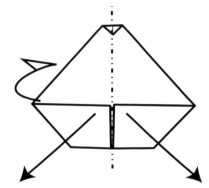

Mountain fold the paper in half. Open out the two corners to form the ears.

7

Balance the head upon the other piece of paper, which is made by folding it in half to form a triangle.

Apatosaurus

Sixty-five million years ago, the animals that lived on Earth were much different from those that live here now. Many were very large, and dinosaurs were among the largest. The **proportions** of the dinosaur called apatosaurus show how the legs and body must have been large and strong to support its great size. These creatures could eat leaves from the tops of tall plants. Their long necks must have been useful. Scientists have thousands of bones from dinosaurs but few clues about how they really looked. Some experts think their skin was brightly colored and patterned. Some may have had scales or even feathers. Decorate your Apatosaurus to show what this creature might have looked like.

1

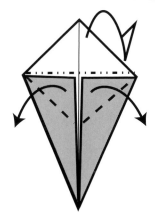

Use two squares of paper 6 inches (15.2 cm) wide or less. If you are using origami paper, start with the white side up. Start with your papers folded to the kite shape. This shape is shown in step three of the origami Ducks. <u>Mountain fold</u> the top corner to the back. Carefully fold the two remaining square corners out.

2

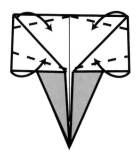

Fold in the four corners of each paper. The top corners should meet the bottom corners.

3

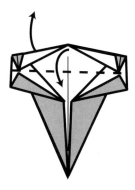

Fold the top area in half. Allow the corner from the underside to come over to the front.

4

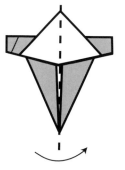

Fold each paper in half.

5

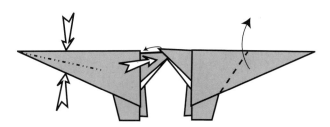

You should have two pieces folded to step number four. Fit the two pieces together by pushing the folded triangular points inside the layers shown. Pinch one end to form the tail.

6

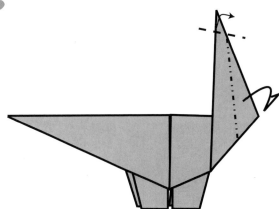

Fold up the end opposite the tail to form the neck. Make the neck narrower by <u>mountain folding</u> the front edge to the back. Fold over the top point to form the head.

Origami Key

1. MOUNTAIN FOLD

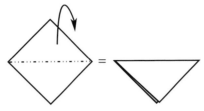

mountain-
fold line

To make a mountain fold, hold the paper so the bottom (white) side is facing up. Fold the top corner back (away from you) to meet the bottom corner.

2. VALLEY FOLD

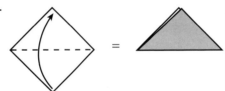

valley-
fold line

To make a valley fold, hold the paper so the white side is facing up. Fold the bottom corner up to meet the top corner.

3. TURN OVER

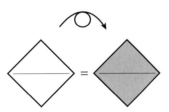

4. ROTATE

5. MOVE or PUSH

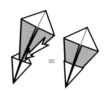

6. CUT

7. FOLD and UNFOLD

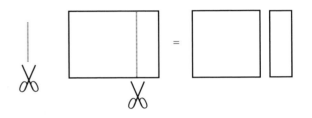

8. DIRECTION ARROW

Glossary

annoying (uh-NOY-ing) Bothering and angering someone.

chrysalis (KRIH-suh-lis) A middle stage in the growth of a butterfly.

culture (KUL-cher) The beliefs, customs, arts, and religions of different groups of people.

discourage (dis-KUHR-ij) To try to keep someone or something from doing a certain act.

grubs (GRUBZ) Insects in the early stage of growth.

hibernate (HY-bur-nayt) To spend the winter sleeping or resting.

mammals (MAM-ulz) Animals that are warm-blooded, breathe oxygen, and give birth to live young.

muzzle (MUZ-uhl) The part of the head of an animal that makes up the nose, mouth, and jaws.

nocturnal (nok-TER-nul) To be active during the night.

personality (per-sun-A-lih-tee) How a person or an animal acts and relates to others.

proportions (pro-POR-shuns) The comparison of sizes and measurements.

revere (rih-VEAR) To regard with respect.

symbols (SIM-bulz) Objects or designs that stand for something important.

Index

Web Sites

To find out more about origami, check out these Web sites:

www.origamido.com
www.origami-usa.org